Daily Devotions

31 Days of Grace:

Grace for Living Among The Thorns

Ginger L. Ilami

31 Days of Grace: Grace for Living Among the Thorns

Cover photo by Ginger L. Ilami with thanks to her son, Isaac, for the loan of his cactus.

ISBN 978-0615943664

Introduction

This is a 31 day devotional focused specifically on discovering what the Bible has to say about God's grace. Each devotion includes a scripture reading, space to paraphrase and personalize the verse, points to consider, questions for digging deeper, and a closing prayer. I would recommend using a journal along with this book so you will have adequate space to write out your paraphrase and answers to questions. It can be helpful to see how your answers change over time when you go through the devotional more than once. My hope and prayer is and that you will discover God's grace as it is manifested in every aspect of your life. Living in God's grace changes everything.

- Ginger L. Ilami-

Other books by Ginger L. Ilami

31 Days of Joy: An Eternity of Rejoicing

31 Days of Grace

2 Corinthians 12:9-10
New International Version 1984 (NIV1984)

9 But he said to me, "My grace is sufficient for you, for my power is made perfect in weakness." Therefore I will boast all the more gladly about my weaknesses, so that Christ's power may rest on me. 10 That is why, for Christ's sake, I delight in weaknesses, in insults, in hardships, in persecutions, in difficulties. For when I am weak, then I am strong.

Paraphrase this scripture (put it into your own words and try to include your name as if God were speaking directly to you):

Living every day in a fallen world is hard. We all struggle with adversities that are frustrating and painful. We suffer at times in our lives from physical, emotional and even spiritual pain. Have you ever felt like you were barely hanging on by your finger nails and that your walk with the Lord would be so much better if life were just a little easier?

These verses give God's reaction to Paul praying three times and asking that God remove the "thorn" from his flesh. Paul suffered from some malady that caused him great torment. Common sense tells us that it would have been better for God to remove it and allow Paul to pursue God's calling in the best of circumstances. Perhaps Paul would have been able to reach more people if he had not been weakened by this suffering. "Wouldn't my walk with God be more successful if I didn't have to deal with . . .?"

God knows our sinful nature and our inclination to depend on our own strength rather than His. How blessed we are that we don't have to live the perfect life to attain salvation. Christ did it for us. How blessed we are that we don't have to die for our sins. Christ did that for us. This is grace, and is cause for us to rejoice through all of eternity! But grace is more than an event occurring in the past. Grace is available to empower us every moment of every day.

God's daily grace is mercy and kindness that exerts a holy influence on us. Grace provides joy, strength, sweetness, and spiritual bounty. God also tells us that His provision is sufficient. His provision of strength is unfailing. Our Heavenly Father does not withhold this power from us. He offers it to us, moment by moment, and all we have to do is accept it. Paul found this grace so powerful in his life that he delighted in his weakness and suffering, because he could then rejoice in the power of God's grace all the more.

God chooses broken vessels to do His work. But He does not leave us to flounder about with an impossible task. Our suffering is useful when it turns us to the source of power that is unfailing. It also demonstrates His grace to all who may see His power in us. We are most useful to God when we are useless to ourselves.

Personal Touch:

What "thorn" are you currently dealing with?

What might be God's purpose for allowing this in your life?

How are you most useful to God through this weakness?

Prayer:

"Dear Heavenly Father, I am struggling with (include your own "thorn"). I thank you that you promise to never leave me or forsake me. I thank you that you provide grace that is sufficient for me. Help me to believe that. I turn my life over to you and ask that you would empower me and that I would be useful to you today. Keep me from self-pity and focus my eyes firmly on Christ. Life may not be pretty right now but I know that you have a purpose and I rest in your faithfulness and your grace. In Jesus' precious name I pray, Amen."

1 Corinthians 15:10
New International Version 1984 (NIV1984)

10 But by the grace of God I am what I am, and his grace to me was not without effect. No, I worked harder than all of them—yet not I, but the grace of God that was with me.

Paraphrase this scripture (put it into your own words and try to include your name as if God were speaking directly to you):

Have you ever felt like a failure? I know I have. It seems that people struggle with either thinking too highly of themselves or too poorly of themselves and sometimes both within the same day. Neither is good, and ultimately they both involve spending a great deal of time and effort thinking about self. In this passage, Paul talks about his view of self. He persecuted the Christians before his encounter with Jesus. If anyone could feel like a failure it was Paul. He could have also taken pride in all the work he then did for Christ. He found the better way.

Humility is not a matter of disliking yourself. Being humble is not thinking of yourself at all. That is what Paul is doing here. Putting away guilt and pride, he looked directly at God, and what God had done in and through him. Grace abounds when guilt and pride are extinguished. It's all about God and His grace, nothing about self.

As a believer, you have been given the grace of God. You are forgiven and there is no sin too big for God. Give Him any guilt you might be hanging on to. When you find yourself focusing too much on self, whether in the positive or negative, remind yourself that you do not want God's grace to be in vain. When we make it all about us it is no longer about God. To be unencumbered and available for God to use, we must be able to say, "not I, but the grace of God that is in me". Allow the rivers of God's grace to flow through you. Don't build a dam called "Me".

Personal Touch:

Do you tend to struggle with thinking too highly or too poorly of yourself (could be both)?

What would your life look like if you gave both over to God and made it all about Him?

What might you do today to remove any "Me" rocks from your river of grace?

Prayer:

"Dear Heavenly Father, thank you for providing your grace to wash away my guilt and my pride. I admit that sometimes (include a "Me" rock) takes my focus from you and puts it on myself. Take this from me. I give it to you. Help me to be washed in your river of grace and to develop true humility so that I will be of great use to you today. In Jesus' name I pray, Amen."

Ephesians 2:8-9
New International Version 1984 (NIV1984)

8 For it is by grace you have been saved, through faith—and this not from yourselves, it is the gift of God— 9 not by works, so that no one can boast.

Paraphrase this scripture (put it into your own words and try to include your name as if God were speaking directly to you):

Salvation by grace is what separates Christianity from all other religions. It is also a very difficult concept for many to grasp. Some people struggle with the idea that God saves us based on the merit of Christ's life, death, and resurrection rather than on our own actions. This is God's plan of salvation. His wrath toward our sin is appeased through Christ's death on our behalf, and the righteousness of Christ's perfect life is imputed to us. All we have to do is believe that Christ paid the penalty for our sin, and we are saved.

An even more difficult concept wrapped up in grace is that, by its nature, grace is not fair. A person can theoretically live a debauched life and believe in Christ on their death bed, and they will go to heaven. They are as saved as the person who believes Christ as a young person and labors all their life as a missionary. This is a stumbling block for many people.

God's plan of salvation is about His glory and His mercy. God knows that even our best will never be good enough, so He provided for us through His great mercy. As for fairness, simply put, we have all earned hell and it is only through His amazing compassion and grace that any are saved.

Unfortunately, even among believers there is often a sense of comparison and competition. It is all too easy to give in to the sinful desire to rank yourself against others. It is also easy to become judgmental and focus on others' visible sins while brushing aside your own invisible ones. God sees and knows all. The only comparison to be made is between yourself and the perfection of Christ. Let go of boasting (even what you keep to yourself), for none of us has a leg to stand on. Let it go and embrace God's grace.

Now, back to that missionary discussed earlier, please understand that there is grace and blessing in a life lived for God and there is reward in heaven. This kind of life shines with love, joy, peace, patience, kindness, goodness, faithfulness, gentleness and self-control. This life is one watered by the very grace of God! Just as God provides for our salvation, He also is the only source of true love and satisfaction.

Personal Touch:

In what ways do you compare yourself to other people?

What impact do these comparisons have on you and your relationship with God?

What can you do today to encourage others rather than tear them down?

Prayer:

"Dear Heavenly Father, thank you for the free gift of salvation that you have provided. I am struck dumb to think that you loved me enough to send your only Son to die for me! I confess that sometimes I can be prideful about (include any prideful thoughts). Fill my life with your grace! May I live a life so rich in your grace that no one could look upon me without seeing you! In Jesus' name I pray, Amen."

2 Peter 3:17-18
New International Version 1984 (NIV1984)

17 Therefore, dear friends, since you already know this, be on your guard so that you may not be carried away by the error of lawless men and fall from your secure position. 18 But grow in the grace and knowledge of our Lord and Savior Jesus Christ. To him be glory both now and forever! Amen.

Paraphrase this scripture (put it into your own words and try to include your name as if God were speaking directly to you):

There are those who seek to distort the word of God. There are people who are teaching falsity and calling it truth. We are to be on our guard against such people. Following the words of men or women over the word of God can make us useless to God. This is a very dangerous situation to toy with. No matter who your pastor is or who you are listening to about spiritual matters, every word they speak must be held up against the word of God in the Bible.

False teaching often tells us exactly what we want to hear. For example, we might want to believe that if we live a godly life we will never suffer. But does believing that make it true? God's word tells us very specifically that Christians will suffer in this life. Following after a lie that we would like to believe will never make it true. You won't lose salvation if you already have it, but you can impede His ability to work in and through you by believing a lie.

So how do you know whether someone is teaching falsity or truth? We are told to grow in the grace and knowledge of our Lord and Savior Jesus Christ. Get into the word of God and learn what it says! We are never to take anyone's teaching over what is said in the Bible. As you seek God in His word you will find His grace to understand and you will grow in your knowledge of Him. When you do find a solid Biblical teacher, rejoice, but never stop testing what they say against scripture.

All glory is to go to God, both now and forever. Keep your eyes always on Him and on His word. Following after men can be a dangerous proposition. If you are saved, the best thing the devil can do is take you out of action or make you ineffectual. Beware! Test every word, keep the glory where it belongs, and grow in the grace and knowledge of our Lord and Savior Jesus Christ!

Personal Touch:

How do you guard against false teaching?

Have you ever convinced yourself of things that are not Biblical?

What is one way you can improve your ability to distinguish truth from lies we like to hear?

Prayer:

"Dear Heavenly Father, thank you for providing us with your word of truth. Guide me and help me to guard against any false teaching I might encounter. Help me to continue to grow in the knowledge of truth, so that I will be ready and able to distinguish right from wrong. May I never convince myself of anything false. May I find complete satisfaction in your word and in your Holy Spirit. In Jesus' name I pray, Amen."

Proverbs 3:34
New International Version 1984 (NIV1984)

34 He mocks proud mockers
but gives grace to the humble.

Paraphrase this scripture (put it into your own words and try to include your name as if God were speaking directly to you):

Today's society is all about pride and all about self. We are told that self-esteem should have nothing to do with the kind of life we lead. Esteem is seen as a person's due simply because they are breathing. I have seen young girls wear tee-shirts saying "It's all about me". In so many ways, being all about self is rewarded and encouraged in our society. God sees things differently.

Those who mock God by living for self will eventually discover the truth. God is very patient, but He will have the final word. God may allow people to live in a world of self-worship and pride but eternity will bear out the truth. That reality will either involve an eternity of separation from God for the unsaved, or loss of blessing for the saved.

It is easy to find ourselves slipping into the position of scorning God and placing ourselves on the throne of life. It happens so easily. "Self" desires the crown that God deserves. It is a constant battle that must be fought from our knees, daily, hourly, moment by moment, placing God on the throne of our life.

When we humble ourselves and allow God to have His rightful place on the throne, God gives us grace. This is grace for salvation as well as grace for functioning and thriving in the world. God gives His unmerited favor to the humble. This is a gift not to be missed! Who's on the throne of your life?

Personal Touch:

What does it look like when you have yourself on the throne of your life?

What does it look like when you have God on the throne of your life?

How can you increase the amount of time God spends on the throne in your life?

Prayer:

"Dear Heavenly Father, thank you for the grace that saved me. Thank you for your grace which sustains me. Too often I allow "self" to climb on the throne of my life. I confess that I have taken over your throne in my life by (include an area of pride or selfishness). I bow before you and ask you to rule over my life. I pray that you would guide me and use me for your eternal purposes. Thank you for (include specific ways in which God has "graced" you). Help me to never take you for granted and to glorify you in all that I do and say. In Jesus' name I pray, Amen."

Philippians 1:7
New International Version 1984 (NIV1984)

7 It is right for me to feel this way about all of you, since I have you in my heart; for whether I am in chains or defending and confirming the gospel, all of you share in God's grace with me.

Paraphrase this scripture (put it into your own words and try to include your name as if God were speaking directly to you):

Nothing will bind you to another person more powerfully than suffering together. Paul felt this way about the Philippian church. The bond he felt was strong because they were with him no matter what his circumstance. Paul describes his feelings toward them as being right and as having value.

Life within the world tends to have very little of this kind of loyalty. In general, people tend to be fickle and like to leave as soon as things get tough or uncomfortable. But God desires a different kind of bond between His people. We are to share in God's grace through the good and through the pain. We are to walk through the blessings and the suffering with those people God places in our lives. We are to share in God's grace no matter the circumstances.

Look around and see who might need to share in God's grace. Together we are so much stronger than apart. Even when separated by distance, we manage better when we know someone is praying for us. Along with the blessings we receive from God, having been prayed over, there is value in knowing that we are not alone. We may not be able to walk with someone in their personal struggle, but we can come alongside of them and offer love and support. We need fellow believers to help us hold up that shield of faith when we are under fire.

Sharing in God's grace will make you vulnerable. You can't have this bond with someone without experiencing some of their pain. But this is God's design. We are to open ourselves up to potential suffering and participate in God's grace because the outcome will ultimately be to God's glory. When we refuse to risk the bonds of suffering with someone we also give up the bonds of joy.

Personal Touch:

Have you ever run away from sharing in God's grace with someone who was struggling? What did that look like?

Have you ever shared in God's grace with someone who was struggling? What did that look like?

Who can you reach out to today? How?

Prayer:

"Dear Heavenly Father, thank you for allowing me to share in your grace through the relationships you have given to me. Thank you for the joy and the pain that you use to grow me, to grow others, and to bring glory to yourself. Help me to not be afraid of being vulnerable. Bring people to me who will share in this and help bear my burdens, and who will allow me to share in theirs. In Jesus' name I pray, Amen."

Jonah 2:7-9
New International Version 1984 (NIV1984)

7 "When my life was ebbing away,
    I remembered you, LORD,
and my prayer rose to you,
    to your holy temple.
8 "Those who cling to worthless idols
    forfeit the grace that could be theirs.
9 But I, with a song of thanksgiving,
    will sacrifice to you.
What I have vowed I will make good.
    Salvation comes from the LORD."

Paraphrase this scripture (put it into your own words and try to include your name as if God were speaking directly to you):

When was the last time you knew what God wanted you to do in a particular situation, but for whatever reason, you chose another path? Are you always obedient to God's Word? Do you allow idols to guide your choices? There is a continual battle going on over who is in control of your life. Jonah chose his own path out of fear. But then what?

Jonah ran from God and found himself in the belly of a great fish. In this deepest pit and in great despair, he remembered God and cried out to Him. His prayer rose all the way to heaven. It took a drastic situation to get Jonah's attention, but when he humbled himself before his Father, God heard his cry. This desperation helped Jonah to remember the great mercy of God and what he gave up in seeking selfish desires.

To "forfeit the grace that could be theirs" is a very powerful statement and should be read slowly and carefully. Jonah learned a very hard lesson about God's economy. He warns others about the folly of seeking anything but what God desires for you. This does not mean that God's path will be easy, but it does mean that it will be littered with God's grace for you. His unmerited favor will fund your act of obedience.

When you find yourself in a pit, whether of your own making or not, remember your Father and know that your prayers will be heard. Follow God's plan and find the grace He provides all along the way. Seeking our own path and our own plan leaves behind the day-to-day logistical grace God desires to lavish upon us. No idol is worth that.

Personal Touch:

Describe a time when you sought your own path rather than God's.

Describe a time when you were obedient to God. What grace did you find there?

What can you do today to be obedient to God's will for you?

Prayer:

"Dear Heavenly Father, thank you for providing your Word as a guide for my life. I confess that I have been disobedient in (include an area of your life that pulls you away from God). May I learn from Jonah's warning that following anything other than you is not worth what I would be giving up. Help me to be obedient and humble myself before you in all things. Thank you for the grace you will provide! In Jesus' name I pray, Amen."

Luke 2:40
New International Version 1984 (NIV1984)

40 And the child grew and became strong; he was filled with wisdom, and the grace of God was upon him.

Paraphrase this scripture (put it into your own words and try to include your name as if God were speaking directly to you):

This is a description of the childhood of Jesus. How many of us would use the same words to tell the story of our early years? This is the only description we have of the growth and development of perfect, sinless humanity. Jesus grew physically and was strong. He also had wisdom. We all "learned" while we grew up but how many can say that their childhood was filled with wisdom? We, as children, demonstrated our fallen nature very clearly in our pride and selfishness, that our parents may have attempted to curb. Christ, however, grew without sin.

The passage continues by saying that the grace of God was upon Him. This is not grace for salvation because Christ did not need salvation. He came to be our salvation. God the Father provided His Son with daily provisional grace. This is such a beautiful picture! The grace of God was upon Him showing God's favor, provision, guidance, and blessing. Does this mean that Christ would never go through hard times? No. Of course Christ would suffer. That was His purpose. But He did it through the guidance and provision of His Heavenly Father, knowing that He was working within the will of His Father.

We can take great comfort from this because God's grace is not just for salvation! As if that were not enough, God also provides His grace for our every need. It is up to us whether we take advantage of what God is providing. Sin and distraction can place walls between us and the abundant living that God desires for His people. Live today with your eyes ever open to see the grace that God is placing before you.

Personal Touch:

How has God given you provisional grace for living recently?

What sometimes prevents you from fully participating in God's daily, provisional grace?

What can you do today to keep your focus on God and His grace?

Prayer:

"*Dear Heavenly Father, I praise you for the sacrifice of your Son for my salvation. I also praise you for placing your grace upon me every day. I admit that (include anything getting in the way) prevents me from fully participating in your daily provisional grace. Help me to live today with eyes that see you and your grace. Give me wisdom to grow and become all that you desire for me. Help my life to be pleasing to you, Father. In Jesus' name I pray, Amen.*"

Romans 3:23-24
New International Version 1984 (NIV1984)

23 for all have sinned and fall short of the glory of God, 24 and are justified freely by his grace through the redemption that came by Christ Jesus.

Paraphrase this scripture (put it into your own words and try to include your name as if God were speaking directly to you):

There is good news and there is bad news. Let's start with the bad news. We have all earned and deserve hell. There is not one of us that can live a perfect, sinless life. Some think that we just need to try our best, or that we just need to be better than the guy down the street, in order to earn heaven. God's standard, however, for getting into heaven is Himself. We have to be as good as God in order to get into heaven. None of us lives up to that benchmark on our own. That's the bad news.

The good news is that Christ Jesus lived the sinless life we could not, and then He died in our place. He took our sin debt on Himself and gave us His righteousness so that we could go to heaven and spend eternity with Him. If we have faith and believe that Christ accomplished this for us we will go to heaven! This is good news, indeed!!

Most likely, you have heard this good news before. It is a glorious thing. But does is impact your daily life? It should. Never forget, dear reader, that even though we are justified freely by His grace, it was purchased at a very dear cost. Always remember what Jesus suffered in order to purchase your freedom from hell. They say that freedom is not free. Well, a price was paid. You, however, were not the one to pay the fee.

What happened at the cross should impact everything you do. Whatever you are facing today, take it to the cross and look at it through the shadow of what Christ has given you. "If Christ suffered and died on the cross for me, then I can surely . . ."

Personal Touch:

How does the gospel story influence your daily life?

How might your life be different if you looked at everything through the prism of what Christ suffered in order to save you?

How can you make what happened on the cross an integral part of your day today?

Prayer:

"Dear Heavenly Father, thank you for saving me! Help me to never forget the horrifying cost that was paid for my salvation. I confess that I get caught up in (include any distractions) and sometimes I forget about the importance of the gospel. Help me to live today in the shadow of the cross. Change me because of what you did. In Jesus' precious name I pray, Amen."

1 Peter 4:10
New International Version 1984 (NIV1984)

10 Each one should use whatever gift he has received to serve others, faithfully administering God's grace in its various forms.

Paraphrase this scripture (put it into your own words and try to include your name as if God were speaking directly to you):

All that we have we owe to God's grace. Without God we would face an eternity in hell. God has saved us from that end and has filled our lives with His grace. He has given us gifts for a purpose. The ways in which we have been blessed, and the talents God has given us, are for the purpose of blessing others.

You might say that you don't have any gifts from God, but that is simply untrue. Upon salvation each person receives a spiritual gift from God, something to aid you in the work He plans for you. But beyond that, even if the gift you have is a positive attitude during a difficult time, that is from God. If you truly look at your life you will find something with which you have been blessed. All that we have, we owe to God and we are meant to be stewards of God's grace, not vaults to store up grace for ourselves.

You are asked to faithfully administer God's grace in its various forms. What you have been given, you are to faithfully pour forth to others. Not just once in a while, when it occurs to you. We need to plan and be strategic with this rather than just letting it happen when it happens. You are to handle the gifts with which you have been graced and serve others in a manner that would be pleasing to God.

As you go through life, and God changes your circumstances, the way you share your gifts and blessings will change as well. Through the lean, hard times and also through the fat and easy times, you are to faithfully administer God's grace. You may dream of the easy times and think that it would be so simple to bless others then. But when you think about it, so much blessing comes from the overflow of God's grace during hard times. It is powerful to see five loaves and two fish multiply right before your eyes as you reach out to someone in faith knowing that you have little to offer materially. If all you have to give today is a hug, find someone who needs one.

Personal Touch:

Describe the talents, gifts and blessings that God has given you.

How can you improve and be more strategic in the use of your gifts?

Who might you share God's grace with today?

Prayer:

"Dear Heavenly Father, thank you for the many blessings you have given me. Help me to be a faithful administrator of what you have given me. Help me to not be stingy with what you have given. Show me who I am to bless today. Help me to not get so caught up in the logistics of my daily life that I miss any opportunity to be gracious to others. Use me today, Lord! In Jesus' name I pray, Amen."

Hebrews 4:16
New International Version 1984 (NIV1984)

16 Let us then approach the throne of grace with confidence, so that we may receive mercy and find grace to help us in our time of need.

Paraphrase this scripture (put it into your own words and try to include your name as if God were speaking directly to you):

Jesus paid the price for our sin and lived the sinless life we cannot live. He took the wrath of God, that we have earned for ourselves, upon Himself. He died and rose again so He could freely give us His righteousness. Because of this we can now approach God's throne of grace. Pause and contemplate this for a moment. We can freely go before the throne of the Creator of the Universe!

Most thrones in history are places where justice or punishment is dispensed. They were approached with great dread and fear. But God's justice has been satisfied. He chose to make His throne one of grace. Oh, thank you, Holy Father! We are told in this verse to approach the throne of grace with confidence. Do you go before your Heavenly Father boldly and with confidence, or do you shrink back? God's grace is a grace that provides for our salvation – once and for all. Approach His throne with confidence, along the path that Jesus provided for us, knowing that this is the desire of your creator and Heavenly Father.

It is before this throne of grace that we receive mercy and find grace to help us in our time of need. God's grace provides for our salvation, but it also provides for our day-to-day needs as we walk the path He has set before us. Have you ever really thought about this? God wants you to confidently come before Him so He can give you mercy and grace to help you though your times of need! Well, ok! So why do we find this so difficult sometimes?

What is holding you back today? Fear? Pride? Self-reliance? An inability to submit? Feeling inadequate? Whatever it is, go confidently before your Father in Heaven and give it all over to Him. He has said that when you do this He will give you mercy and you will find grace to help you in your time of need. Why would you hold back? It is God's fervent desire that you allow Him to help you with your every need! What are you allowing to get between you and your King?

Personal Touch:

What gets in the way of your approaching the throne of grace with confidence?

What is one thing you can change about your prayer life today that would incorporate what is said in this verse?

Describe an experience you have had with God's mercy and grace.

Prayer:

"Dear Heavenly Father, thank you for providing for my salvation through your son, Jesus Christ. Thank you for your throne of grace and for allowing me to live in Christ. I give to you (include whatever might be hindering your approaching the throne of grace). Fill me up and may your grace shine forth through me. Help me with (include a need that you are experiencing). May your grace provide for me and guide me through this valley. I praise you that you are a God who not only cares about my every moment in life but one who desires to help me with every need. With humble adoration and in Jesus' precious name I pray, Amen."

John 1:14
New International Version 1984 (NIV1984)

14 The Word became flesh and made his dwelling among us. We have seen his glory, the glory of the One and Only, who came from the Father, full of grace and truth.

Paraphrase this scripture (put it into your own words and try to include your name as if God were speaking directly to you):

It is so easy to gloss over verses like this one. Yes, Jesus became a man, came to earth, and died for me. We've heard this a million times. Great, what next? How does this help me with my life today? What is being said here, however, does have meaning for your everyday life.

First of all, Jesus underwent a transition, became flesh, and made his dwelling among people. Before this, God's "dwelling place" was in the tabernacle. The tabernacle was all about the law and was a foreshadowing of what was to come. In the tabernacle, only the High Priest could enter the Holy of Holies and then only once a year, and he did it with fear for his very life. Jesus changed this. He came and brought grace for us so that we could dwell with Him, not just near Him. Think about that for a moment.

Next, the witnesses saw the glory of God in Jesus. They knew that He was the only Son of God and that He was sent by the Father. The Father sent Him, not empty and needy, but full of grace and truth. This is exactly what we need for salvation and what we need for living every day. He is the perfect, acceptable substitute for our death sentence. And once we accept His intercession, He dwells within us in order to grace our every moment.

Finally, while the tabernacle and the sacrificial system were shadows pointing to God's plan for salvation, Jesus came full of truth and was our salvation. He was fully able to guide and instruct us in God's truth, and He came as the fulfillment of all that the Old Testament system of worship revealed.

Does the fact that God came to dwell with you, providing fullness of grace and truth, impact you at all? Perhaps it is something that you should revisit once in a while. When the thorns of life begin to prick, when life hurts and you need grace, truth, and companionship, Jesus is where you will find what you need.

Personal Touch:

What area of your life are you struggling to turn over to God?

What might change if you allowed God control in all areas of your life? What prevents you?

Where do you need God's grace most today?

Prayer:

"Dear Heavenly Father, thank you for moving us from the law into grace. Thank you for the sacrifice that you made to save me. Help me to remember that what Jesus did for me impacts, not just my past and my eternity, but also my present. Give me grace to live today and help me to keep your truth in the forefront of my mind. In Jesus name I pray, Amen."

2 Corinthians 4:14-16
New International Version 1984 (NIV1984)

14 because we know that the one who raised the Lord Jesus from the dead will also raise us with Jesus and present us with you in his presence. 15 All this is for your benefit, so that the grace that is reaching more and more people may cause thanksgiving to overflow to the glory of God.

16 Therefore we do not lose heart. Though outwardly we are wasting away, yet inwardly we are being renewed day by day.

Paraphrase this scripture (put it into your own words and try to include your name as if God were speaking directly to you):

What keeps you going every day? Have you ever noticed that what you think about events in life determines how you will react to events in life? A trial seems so much harder when you believe that it will produce nothing positive. These verses are talking about what kept the apostles going, and that was the thought of the resurrection. They knew that just as Jesus was raised from the dead, so they would be raised from the dead and be with Christ.

Through the grace of God we are adopted into His family and into resurrection and eternity with Him. This should change how you look at your life, especially your trials. To struggle with no purpose is defeating. To struggle with a purpose invigorates your soul, draws you closer to God, and gives reason for thanksgiving.

In verse 16, it says that they were wasting away outwardly but being renewed inwardly. We are all struggling to live in an ugly world. Life is hard. We are all physically declining. But God is growing us through all of it, and even as we are afflicted outwardly in our body, we are becoming more dynamic spiritually.

So what keeps you going every day? Focus on what God is doing in and through you as you face your trials. If you don't know what God has planned, then kick in the 'trust thrusters' and wait expectantly to see what He will do. And above all, remember that the one who raised Jesus will also raise you, and you will spend eternity in His presence. While you wait for that day, allow God's grace to renew you on the inside. What is keeping you going today?

Personal Touch:

What makes getting through the day tough for you?

How do you see God renewing you day by day?

What can you do today to focus more on heavenly glory than your earthly decline?

Prayer:

"Dear Heavenly Father, thank you for the grace through which you are providing for my resurrection and eternity with you. It is easy to forget what you have done and are doing for me, and I am sorry. Help me to remember and keep my focus on the heavenly glory rather than the struggles I face here. Make me spiritually vigorous and always grateful. In Jesus' name I pray, Amen."

Ephesians 1:4-8
New International Version 1984 (NIV1984)

4 For he chose us in him before the creation of the world to be holy and blameless in his sight. In love 5 he predestined us to be adopted as his sons through Jesus Christ, in accordance with his pleasure and will 6 to the praise of his glorious grace, which he has freely given us in the One he loves. 7 In him we have redemption through his blood, the forgiveness of sins, in accordance with the riches of God's grace 8 that he lavished on us with all wisdom and understanding.

Paraphrase this scripture (put it into your own words and try to include your name as if God were speaking directly to you):

"Choose me! Choose me!" Have you ever said or thought these words? I know that I have. We all desire to belong and to be loved. Well, there is good news. As a believer in Christ, you were chosen, in love, before the world was even created! As a result of this, you have been set apart as the adopted child of the God of the Universe. You have been redeemed and forgiven, and you belong to God. Why did He do it? It was in accordance with His pleasure and will.

God has freely given us His grace and salvation through our Savior, Jesus Christ. Through His great wisdom and understanding He has lavished us with grace. Even though the situation of sin may have seemed hopeless, God had a plan to not only satisfy His need to punish sin, as was necessary, but to save us and to bring glory to Himself in the process.

If you are a believer, God has chosen you and lavishes you with His glorious grace. Believe it and live it. Never demean yourself by seeking the world's approval. You are a chosen child of God. Live like it!

If you are not a believer, or are not sure if you are a believer, then God is anxiously waiting for the moment when He can lavish you with His glorious grace. If you are in this unbelieving category, the prayer at the end of this devotional is a prayer of salvation you can speak directly to God. Believe in what God has done for you and you can know that God has chosen you!

Personal Touch:

Do you feel loved and like you belong to God? What might prevent you from feeling this?

Will the fact that you were chosen according to His pleasure change how you live your life? How?

How would your life look if you always truly believed you belong to the God of the Universe? Be specific.

Prayer:

"Dear Heavenly Father, I come to you confessing that I am a sinner. I am in need of a Savior because I cannot ever be good enough on my own (no one can). Thank you for sending Jesus to take my place and pay the price required for my sin. I believe that Jesus died for me and rose again so that I could go to heaven and spend eternity with you. Thank you for forgiveness of my sins, thank you for redeeming me from slavery to sin, and thank you for lavishing your grace upon me. In Jesus' name I pray, Amen."

Colossians 4:5-6
New International Version 1984 (NIV1984)

5 Be wise in the way you act toward outsiders; make the most of every opportunity. 6 Let your conversation be always full of grace, seasoned with salt, so that you may know how to answer everyone.

Paraphrase this scripture (put it into your own words and try to include your name as if God were speaking directly to you):

Do these verses ever cause you to wince just a bit? It is not easy to always behave and speak the way that God would have us. This is especially difficult when we don't agree with someone. But God wants us to seek Him and grow in Him so that we will be wise in how we behave toward those with whom we might disagree.

We are to make the most of every opportunity placed before us so that seeds are planted. Now this doesn't mean that every conversation is to be about grace. But every conversation needs to be full of grace. How we behave and how we speak (no matter what the topic) we are to exude the grace of God. There should be something about us that is attractive and leaves a good taste in people's mouths-especially when these are people with whom we disagree.

We are ambassadors in a foreign country. We need God's wisdom and grace to guide us in behaving in a way that is, frankly, not natural. Our natural inclination is to argue and defend, or simply ignore, when encountering someone who disagrees with our position. God says that when we seek His wisdom and let His grace temper our behavior and our words we will be able to answer with wisdom and love.

Take a new position today. Make the most of every opportunity you have. Love everyone with God's love so that your conversation will be full of grace. Try again with people you have already behaved poorly toward. Be full of grace in everything you do today.

Personal Touch:

What situations are most difficult for you to let your conversation be full of grace? Why?

What do you need to let go of in order to be full of grace in these situations?

What can you do differently today to help temper your words with grace?

Prayer:

"Dear Heavenly Father, thank you for making your wisdom available to help me with these kinds of situations. I give you my pride and pray that you will give me your love for others so that I will be able to show your grace and be a tasty seasoning to someone today. Help me to make use of every opportunity you place before me. In Jesus' name I pray, Amen."

Hebrews 13:9-10
New International Version 1984 (NIV1984)

9 Do not be carried away by all kinds of strange teachings. It is good for our hearts to be strengthened by grace, not by ceremonial foods, which are of no value to those who eat them. 10 We have an altar from which those who minister at the tabernacle have no right to eat.

Paraphrase this scripture (put it into your own words and try to include your name as if God were speaking directly to you):

The book of Hebrews deals with what a struggle it was for Jews to let go of the Old Testament Mosaic order. They had to accept a new way to approach God after the death of the Messiah. Put yourself in their shoes. A massive shift had to take place in their thinking. Salvation through faith in Christ has not changed. Old Testament believers simply had faith in a Messiah that was to come. After the cross, our faith looks back on what has already happened. But they needed to switch from the Levitical priesthood to having Christ as their final, eternal High Priest.

You may look at these verses and think that they don't really apply to you. You probably haven't had a great deal of issues with ceremonial foods. But just as the Jews had to struggle with a change in how they approached God, pre-Messiah versus post-Messiah, we also have to deal with a change in thinking. Does any of your pre-salvation thinking influence your post-salvation life?

When you switch from a works-based life to a life of grace it is a huge leap. It is a switch that we all have to make. It is easy to become a believer and still hang on to old habits of self-reliance and depending on your own works to please God in some way. Take a good look at your life. What "ceremonial foods" are you still hanging on to? What part of your life are you not giving over to God's grace?

We are blessed to live in a time when we can look back and see God's plan of grace fulfilled in the death and resurrection of Jesus Christ. "It is good for our hearts to be strengthened by grace". Where are you seeking strength? If it is in anything other than God's grace, then it is of no ultimate value. Our "alter" is Jesus Christ and all that we need to live the life God ordained for us is found in God's grace. Come to Christ with empty hands and His grace will fill them.

Personal Touch:

What area of your life is the most difficult to completely turn over to God?

What is the difference between working to earn God's favor and doing good works that God wants you to do?

Describe a time that God's grace strengthened your heart.

Prayer:

"Dear Heavenly Father, thank you for saving me. Thank you for putting up with me. I know that I am a sinner and I pray that your grace would fill me and strengthen me for the good works you desire me to accomplish. Lord, fill me so full of your grace that there is no room for my sinfulness or my inclination to rely on myself. I come with empty hands and pray that all that I do in this life will only point others to you. In Jesus' name I pray, Amen."

James 4:4-7
New International Version 1984 (NIV1984)

4 You adulterous people, don't you know that friendship with the world is hatred toward God? Anyone who chooses to be a friend of the world becomes an enemy of God. 5 Or do you think Scripture says without reason that the spirit he caused to live in us envies intensely? 6 But he gives us more grace. That is why Scripture says:
  "God opposes the proud
  but gives grace to the humble."
7 Submit yourselves, then, to God. Resist the devil, and he will flee from you.

Paraphrase this scripture (put it into your own words and try to include your name as if God were speaking directly to you):

        There is nothing like some spiritual adultery to start the day! Wow! James does not pull any punches here. If you are friends with the world you are unfaithful to God and are an enemy of God. In other words, toying with worldly thinking and worldly behavior sets you in opposition to God. It may seem fun and entertaining for a time, but not for long. This passage also states that God is set against the proud. Wow! You might not see yourself as a "friend of the world" but who has not struggled with pride?
        Thank the Lord, He does not leave it there. We are also told how to avoid such disastrous situations. God provides just what we need-His grace. Not only does He provide His grace, He gives us more grace. What a beautiful picture! Here we are spiritually adulterous in our interactions with the world, prideful and selfish, but God gives us more grace than that which pulls us away from Him. What is in the world can never outdo the grace He offers to draw us closer to Him.
        Verse seven includes a command to submit to God. This is not a suggestion, it is a command. Submission to the world (for that is what it is to play with that which is not of God) draws the devil close and keeps him near. Submission to God, placing yourself under His authority, not only deals with pride, but causes the devil to flee. To submit to God is to be humble and God gives grace to the humble.
        Which position will you choose? Will you humbly bow before the God of the Universe (who offers more grace than is necessary to

overcome the world), or will you continue to bow before the world (which desires to destroy you)? Or thirdly, will you bow before a mirror and worship yourself and your own "needs" and desires (and stand in opposition to God)? It is a choice we make every day.

Personal Touch:

In what ways are you friends with the world?

Where do you struggle with pride?

What choice will you make today that will help you submit to God and close the door on the world and on pride?

Prayer:

"Dear Heavenly Father, I confess that (include areas of pride and worldly involvement) places me in opposition to you. Help me to submit to you in all things. I know that you desire good for me and that letting go and resting in your ultimate plans is for my best and for your glory. I know that when I seek you I will find you. I'm seeking you today! In Jesus' name I pray, Amen."

1 Peter 1:13
New International Version 1984 (NIV1984)

13 Therefore, prepare your minds for action; be self-controlled; set your hope fully on the grace to be given you when Jesus Christ is revealed.

Paraphrase this scripture (put it into your own words and try to include your name as if God were speaking directly to you):

Keep your eyes on the prize! As Christians we live in a very hostile environment. We are told in scripture that we will face trials and tribulations. This passage tells us how to get ready for what will be a bumpy ride.

We are to prepare our minds for action. Just as an athlete prepares their body for competition, we are to prepare our minds for the battles to come. This is all about knowing doctrine. We must know what the word of God says. We must be reading the Bible, studying the Bible, and being taught the Bible. It is vitally important to have daily time in the word and regular Church attendance where you are taught and challenged in the word. Bible study classes are also very helpful because you can have dialogue and interaction with teachers and other believers.

This verse also tells us to be self-controlled. It is important to be diligent and strongly focused on your growth in the knowledge of God. We need to separate ourselves from anything that hinders our spiritual growth. Be thoughtful here, because it is often the hard things in life that cause us to grow closer to God.

There is a tough race to be run. Life is messy, and sometimes we find ourselves running through the swamp. It is even harder to run when you are hindered by lack of knowledge, or when you are weighted down by baggage such as addiction or unforgiveness. Also, there will be people trying to steer you off course. There will be offers of delights, tempting you to stop. Now is the time to gird your mind for action. Don't be unprepared!

Set your mind on the prize! The race is hard! Utilize the grace that strengthens you and keep your focus on the grace that is to come. One day this will all be over. One day we will experience ultimate sanctification when we are delivered fully from sin. We will have complete blessedness in an eternity with Christ. It will be worth it! Especially if we have run a good race and get to hear God say,

"Well done my good and faithful servant"! Spend less time looking at the muck you are running through and more time looking at the face of your Savior beckoning you forward!

Personal Touch:

Is there anything that you are carrying that is hindering your ability to run the race well?

What does your current spiritual workout look like?

What can you do today to step up your spiritual training?

Prayer:

"Dear Heavenly Father, thank you for never leaving me to run this race alone. I know that I am carrying (include anything that is hindering your ability to run the race), and I know that it is keeping me from running well. Lord, I give that to you. Help me to let it go and help me to overcome the urge to pick it up again. I praise you that there is freedom in you! Guide me and motivate me in stepping up my spiritual training. Help me to grow in the knowledge of you so that I will be well prepared for what is to come. Keep my eyes on the prize! In Jesus' name I pray, Amen."

John 1:15-17
New International Version 1984 (NIV1984)

15 John testifies concerning him. He cries out, saying, "This was he of whom I said, 'He who comes after me has surpassed me because he was before me.'" 16 From the fullness of his grace we have all received one blessing after another. 17 For the law was given through Moses; grace and truth came through Jesus Christ.

Paraphrase this scripture (put it into your own words and try to include your name as if God were speaking directly to you):

Here again, we have the comparison of the law and Christ. John the Baptist testifies that Jesus is the Messiah. The law was given through Moses and provided a picture of grace. Jesus came and was grace.

Not only was He grace for us, but He came overflowing with grace. God is described as overflowing with various things in the Bible because He desires to share what He is with us. Our cup is to overflow. God desires to share His grace with us-grace for salvation and grace for living the life He gives us. From that comes one blessing after another.

Does this mean that all will be rainbows and unicorns from here on? No. But do not discount the blessings of God. He wants to give us abundant living that is filled to overflowing with His blessings. Sometimes God's blessings come with trouble and suffering. Sometimes the trouble and suffering are the blessing. God knows what is required for others to see Him in you. He also knows what is required for you to grow so that you can become what He knows you will never be without some refining. Then, there are those times where we get in the way of God's blessings, because we think we know the best way to get what we think we need. There are also times when we are being blessed and we just fail to notice and appreciate.

God is overflowing with grace because He wants you to be filled. He does not make it difficult to find or to enjoy His grace. Jesus is ready to pour it out on you. Just ask.

Personal Touch:

What does it mean in your life that God wants to pour what He is into you?

Describe God's most recent blessings in your life. Which blessings came through suffering?

What might be impeding God's ability to bless you? What part do you play?

Prayer:

"Dear Heavenly Father, I praise you for being so kind and good. I am thankful that you, and your blessings, are not hidden from me. I confess that (include things that get in the way of your receiving or enjoying God's blessings) gets between me and your desires for me. Help me to seek, recognize, and appreciate all that you do for and through me. In Jesus name I pray, Amen."

Romans 5:1-2
New International Version 1984 (NIV1984)

1 Therefore, since we have been justified through faith, we have peace with God through our Lord Jesus Christ, 2 through whom we have gained access by faith into this grace in which we now stand. And we rejoice in the hope of the glory of God.

Paraphrase this scripture (put it into your own words and try to include your name as if God were speaking directly to you):

Our faith in God is based upon our dependence on Him to provide that which we could never earn-salvation. Through our faith we are justified and are declared to stand in the righteousness that Christ provides. Because of this, we have peace, grace, and hope.

The peace described here is not as much a feeling but rather a status. The wrath of God has been appeased. God's perfect justice demands payment for our sinfulness. In His perfect love He provided the payment through the death and resurrection of His Son. Therefore, we have a new relationship with God. While we were once enemies, we are now at peace. The truly amazing part of this is that not only are we no longer enemies, but that we are now His friends!

Next, our justification through Christ provides us with access to His grace. Here God's grace is described as "grace in which we now stand". The idea that we are standing in this grace gives the picture that we are now able to stand because our debt has been paid. Does this mean that we live a guiltless life? No. But positionally, God sees us through the righteousness that Christ has provided. Temporally, we live with our old sin nature and must continually seek God's gracious provision to find the way to escape temptation.

Standing in grace also denotes a position of readiness to act. If God had no use for us here on Earth He would save us, and then take us straight into heaven. God has provided grace for us to fulfill His ultimate plan for humanity.

You play a part in that plan, and God gives you grace to carry it out. What an amazing thought! And in all of this, we rejoice because we have hope (Biblically that is a certainty) that we will see the glory of God! We will see the glory of God!!

Personal Touch:

What does being at peace with God look like in your life? What needs to change?

Do you live as though you stand before God with your sins paid for in full? What sins are you hanging on to and why?

How might you live today in a state of readiness to partake in God's grace and be a part of God's ultimate plan?

Prayer:

"Dear Heavenly Father, thank you for providing me with justification which leads to peace, daily grace and hope. I do not deserve it, but you chose me and saved me! I know that (include anything that interferes) sometimes gets in the way of my living with peace, grace, and hope. Help me to show others your peace, to stand ready in your grace, and to rejoice in your hope of glory. In Jesus' name I pray, Amen."

2 Corinthians 6:1-2
New International Version 1984 (NIV1984)

1 As God's fellow workers we urge you not to receive God's grace in vain. 2 For he says,

"In the time of my favor I heard you,
and in the day of salvation I helped you."

I tell you, now is the time of God's favor, now is the day of salvation.

Paraphrase this scripture (put it into your own words and try to include your name as if God were speaking directly to you):

It is time to seize the day! It is time to make your life count. Life is unpredictable and we have no idea what tomorrow might bring. What vanity to have spent your life gathering trophies that will ultimately have no value. What loss to have lived your life in relentless pursuit of solitary pleasure that is fleeting. When a Christian lives like this it is "to receive God's grace in vain".

It is God's desire for us to live a life of grace that will draw others to know of His grace and salvation. We are to be instruments of God. Right now is the time to seize the day and live a life of purpose. Just as God had a day of favor and salvation for us, we are to be tools to spread the word. Let others know that today is the day! Who knows what their future might bring.

We are God's fellow workers so don't forget the work part. What greater pleasure can there be than to be used by God to spread the gospel? What greater delight is there than to play a small part in helping someone draw closer to God? God is ultimately in charge of bringing others to Himself. He does, however, allow us to be used by Him for His glory. What a privilege!

Don't be afraid, and don't think that you have to have a perfect life to be useful as a witness. God has given you struggles and a life story that He knows someone close to you needs to hear. When God gives us joy and victory (sometimes through pain and suffering) He already knows who He wants you to share it with. Be ready because today is the day!

Personal Touch:

What do you fear most about being a fellow worker in Christ?

What would your life look like if you did not have these fears?

What one thing can you do today to seize the day and allow God's grace to flow from you and into someone else?

Prayer:

"Dear Heavenly Father, thank you for your day of favor and salvation for me. Thank you for giving my life eternal purpose. I confess that (include any fears you might have) prevents me from more actively spreading the gospel. Help me to give these concerns to you. Help me to be open to the opportunities you place in my path to share what you have done in my life. Don't let me walk away from anyone who needs what you have given me. In Jesus' name I pray, Amen."

Ephesians 2:6-8
New International Version 1984 (NIV1984)

6 And God raised us up with Christ and seated us with him in the heavenly realms in Christ Jesus, 7 in order that in the coming ages he might show the incomparable riches of his grace, expressed in his kindness to us in Christ Jesus. 8 For it is by grace you have been saved, through faith—and this not from yourselves, it is the gift of God—

Paraphrase this scripture (put it into your own words and try to include your name as if God were speaking directly to you):

Christ has accomplished all that is needed for our salvation. We, as believers, are already seen by God as being dead to sin and raised up with Christ. Our eternity with our Savior is complete and is essentially a done deal. We must still struggle through this life here on earth, but our future with Him is certain.

Because of this, we can have hope! Other religions of the world are all based in uncertainty. People often live life never knowing how eternity will turn out. Were they good enough? Did they sacrifice enough? Were they devout enough? Will their "god" change his mind? They will never know until it is too late and will, therefore, live a life of fear and uncertainty.

With God, it is all based on the incomparable riches of His grace. What a relief! I would much rather trust in the unchanging God of the Universe than in my own emotion-driven, sinful self. I am saved by faith that was planted by God, ignited by God, and is assured by God. And from this solid position we will bring forth good works based on our being a new creation in Christ rather than in an attempt to become something we can never achieve on our own.

Focus on the words used in this passage: riches of His grace, kindness to us, gift of God. He has done everything for you through the incomparable riches of His grace. His grace for you is never ending. His grace is expressed in kindness and is a gift that you can never earn. Rest in what God has done for you and thank Him for His kindness and for the ultimate gift of an eternity with Him. Depend on what God's grace will do for you today.

Personal Touch:

In what do you place your hope? How does that change how you live your life?

Describe God's grace and kindness working in your life recently.

How has God provided His unending grace for you through the tough times?

Prayer:

"Dear Heavenly Father, thank you for basing my salvation on your reliability rather than on my own. I confess that (include what causes you to doubt His kindness) sometimes causes me to doubt your love for me. Help me to give this to you and to rest in your unending grace and kindness-even when that includes difficult times. Help me to trust you no matter what situation you allow in my life. Let my life demonstrate your unending grace. In Jesus' gracious name I pray, Amen."

2 Timothy 2:1-3
New International Version 1984 (NIV1984)

1 You then, my son, be strong in the grace that is in Christ Jesus. 2 And the things you have heard me say in the presence of many witnesses entrust to reliable men who will also be qualified to teach others. 3 Endure hardship with us like a good soldier of Christ Jesus.

Paraphrase this scripture (put it into your own words and try to include your name as if God were speaking directly to you):

Being strong in Christ is very different from what our society calls strength. We are told by the world that to be strong we must develop self-reliance, self-satisfaction, and do all we can to become self-sustaining. In God's economy, the more room "self" takes up in one's life the less room there is for God.

Ironically, to be strong in the grace of Christ Jesus involves weakness and dying to self. The more we rely on ourselves the less room there is for God's grace to strengthen us. To be filled with grace is to be filled with Christ. These are easy things to say but tough to live out. Our old-sin-nature likes to keep our focus on self. But how do you die to self? How do you stop being self-reliant and become God-reliant? How do you allow yourself to be filled with Christ and His grace?

Ultimately, the answer is in trust. You cannot let go of self until you trust God to take care of you. It's like falling back and trusting someone to catch you. There is much that can keep you from letting go. Faith in God and trusting Him with everything in your life will make you very strong in the "grace that is in Christ Jesus". We all begin with trusting in the small things. Then, as we learn that God is trustworthy we are better able to trust in larger issues. God is training us as soldiers. Just as a soldier must train his body to be physically strong, so we must train ourselves to let go and be strengthened in Him rather than in ourselves.

Does this mean that we just sit back and never actively do anything? This should be the most active thing that we do each day. Actively seek God in His word, in prayer, in fellowship. Seek His will for your life each day. Trusting God to strengthen you to endure hardship is a constant shifting of focus off of your desires and on to God's. It is when we let it go and let Him lead that we are truly strong.

50

Personal Touch:

Where in your life do you tend to be self-reliant?

What would it look like if you gave that area of your life over to God?

What step can you take today that would increase your God focus and decrease your self-focus?

Prayer:

"Dear Heavenly Father, I praise you that I can be strong in the grace that is in Christ Jesus. Thank you for not leaving me alone to struggle through without help. I admit that _(include an area of self-focus)_ is an area where I struggle with allowing you to be my Lord and King. Help me to trust you and show me ways to be more about you and less about me. In Jesus' name I pray, Amen."

Romans 5:17
New International Version 1984 (NIV1984)

17 For if, by the trespass of the one man, death reigned through that one man, how much more will those who receive God's abundant provision of grace and of the gift of righteousness reign in life through the one man, Jesus Christ.

Paraphrase this scripture (put it into your own words and try to include your name as if God were speaking directly to you):

This is a wonderful comparison of Adam, through whom sin entered the world, and Christ, through whom sin was conquered. Through Adam we have all sinned and are born as sinners. Where Adam's disobedience condemned us, Christ's obedience saved us. This is not, however, a comparison of equals. The power of sin through Adam is not the equal opposite of God's grace.

God hates sin and God loves grace. This verse tells us that not only has God dealt with sin, but He is giving an abundant provision of grace to those who believe. There is more grace given than just what is required to cover our guilt. God is good and He is sharing that goodness with us through His grace. Our Heavenly Father could merely restore humanity to the Garden of Eden. He is, however, giving us far more than that for our eternity in heaven.

On Earth, we are more than just pardoned from our sin. We are like Joseph in Egypt. We are not just saved but are elevated through God's grace. We have more than just freedom from death. We have been given abundant grace to reign in life. For "how much more will those who receive God's abundant provision of grace and of the gift of righteousness reign in life through the one man, Jesus Christ".

There is so much more that God desires to give you through His wonderful grace. Death no longer reigns in your life. Live as if that were true, because it is! Live your life out of the abundant provision of grace He is giving you!

Personal Touch:

How does it change your life to know that God is giving you more grace than just what is necessary to save you?

Where do you find God's grace if your life is full of pain and struggle?

How do you partake in God's daily abundant grace when life is hard?

Prayer:

"Dear Heavenly Father, thank you for providing abundant grace so that I may reign in life through Jesus Christ. I praise you for your overwhelming goodness. Please help me to keep our relationship as the priority in my life so that I will live within the grace that you are giving. Right now (include something that is troubling you) has been really tough. I give that to you right now. Your will be done. I thank you for giving me the grace to get through and the grace to grow and influence others positively through this trial. Grow me! In Jesus' name I pray, Amen."

2 Corinthians 8:7-9
New International Version 1984 (NIV1984)

7 But just as you excel in everything—in faith, in speech, in knowledge, in complete earnestness and in your love for us—see that you also excel in this grace of giving. 8 I am not commanding you, but I want to test the sincerity of your love by comparing it with the earnestness of others. 9 For you know the grace of our Lord Jesus Christ, that though he was rich, yet for your sakes he became poor, so that you through his poverty might become rich.

Paraphrase this scripture (put it into your own words and try to include your name as if God were speaking directly to you):

God provides so much for those who follow Him. Through God's grace we receive much more than we deserve. And with what God has given us we are to give to others. No one has given more than Jesus. He gave up the riches of heaven, not just to become a man, but to become a poor man. He lived and died in financial poverty. He was tortured and suffered and died on a cross, though He was innocent. He did all of this for our gain.

In this passage we are asked to excel in the grace of giving because we are living every day through the charity of Christ. All that we have spiritually, physically, and, yes, financially, is because of our Lord Jesus Christ. A test of our love and faith is to see how we are doing in the grace of giving. Your act of faith and obedience in giving to others will not go unnoticed by God.

We should all be giving something financially to support God's work, but "giving" doesn't mean only financial giving. Most of us have gone through tough times and know what it is to be the one who could use a bit of Godly charity. Giving financially is important but it is not the only way we can give. Giving of your time, your labor, and your love to someone in need can be a tremendous help and testimony.

Get creative and think of ways to bless others around you every day. A smile and a word of encouragement to a check-out clerk can make their day. Prayer is a wonderful way to give to others. Get creative, and notice that you will often experience more blessing as the giver than as the receiver.

Personal Touch:

What have you received from God?

In what ways do you already excel in the grace of giving?

What new and creative ways of giving can you add to your giving portfolio?

Prayer:

"Dear Heavenly Father, I praise you for all that you give me every day. Thank you for the opportunity to be a giver too. Open my eyes to new ways and daily opportunities to give so that others will be blessed. Help me to think personally, financially, civically, within and outside of my church. Broaden my grace giving horizons so that you will be glorified. I thank you in advance for the blessings that this giving will bring into my own life. In Jesus' name I pray, Amen."

Titus 2:11-12
New International Version 1984 (NIV1984)

11 For the grace of God that brings salvation has appeared to all men. 12 It teaches us to say "No" to ungodliness and worldly passions, and to live self-controlled, upright and godly lives in this present age,

Paraphrase this scripture (put it into your own words and try to include your name as if God were speaking directly to you):

Here we go again. A list of the things we should not do and a list of the things we should do-just what so many people think that the Bible is all about. How many can you check off? Be careful. Let's take a moment and look a little closer. This is much more than a to-do list.

First of all, the grace of God brings salvation for all people, Jew and gentile. But the purpose of His gospel is more than just saving us from hell. The grace of God is also very practical and useful for daily living. We are saved through no act of our own, but that same grace instructs us in how to live in this age. It draws us into godly living. God provides help for living in this sin-filled world. Our behavior is to be founded on right principles that, without grace, we would be unable to fathom. And the more we grow in God's grace, the more we see our own filth and understand the enormity of what God is doing for us.

Just as a good parent uses various methods to train children in what is expected of them, God, through His grace, shows us how to live. His grace teaches us to turn away from ungodliness and worldly passions. "Ungodliness" describes our heart and "worldly passions" describe the actions that are brought out of an ungodly heart. God's grace shows us His holiness so that we can discern our own ungodly heart and the sin it brings forth. This compassionate action of God can save us from so much pain and suffering! Are you willing to listen?

God's grace shows us how to live thoughtfully. We are to slow down and use caution and self-control. We are to behave uprightly toward other people and have an active relationship with God our Father. We have been given an instruction book for living called The Holy Bible, and through His grace God teaches us how to manage in a very hostile environment. Rather than just giving us a check list,

God gives us Himself. He never leaves us alone. His grace is present at every moment to guide us and protect us. Put away the check list and begin the relationship.

Personal Touch:

Describe your current relationship with your Heavenly Father.

How does your intimacy or lack of intimacy with God effect how you live?

What will you do today to deepen your relationship with God?

Prayer:

"Dear Heavenly Father, thank you for being personal and caring about my daily life. Thank you for giving me grace for living through our relationship. Help me to deepen our relationship so that your grace can be my guide for living in a hostile world. Remove anything that gets in the way of our relationship. In Jesus' name I pray, Amen."

2 Peter 1:2
New International Version 1984 (NIV1984)

2 Grace and peace be yours in abundance through the knowledge of God and of Jesus our Lord.

Paraphrase this scripture (put it into your own words and try to include your name as if God were speaking directly to you):

One of the big questions in life is how to find peace. How many truly peaceful people do you know? How many people do you know who should be peaceful but aren't? Perhaps you thought that you had peace, but then something happened and your world was shaken to the core. This verse tells us exactly where to find peace.

Grace and peace are very often paired together and it is more than just a simple greeting. Through God's grace we initially find Christ, and then through our growing relationship with Christ we find ever increasing grace for living. With grace comes peace. The key to peace is in our knowledge of God and of Jesus our Lord, and of the grace He provides.

It is through our knowledge of Him that God provides all that we need for life and godliness. Submitting to God as the authority in your life, through the study of His word, and through a strong prayer connection, God will abundantly provide all that you need. Of course this does not mean that life will be without pain. But we will know that God is at work when we have abundant grace and peace through a time of suffering. Other people will see that God is at work in your life as well. This grace and peace sets us apart from the world.

It is our job to build intimacy with God. He is always ready and waiting for you. He will then provide grace and peace, and it will be plentiful. God does not give us answers to every question we have, but He gives us all that we need. Grace and peace be yours in abundance.

Personal Touch:

Describe how grace and peace are present, or lacking, in your life currently.

How might you increase the impact of God's grace and peace in your life (according to this verse)?

What will you do today to increase your knowledge of and intimacy with God and Jesus Christ your Lord?

Prayer:

"Dear Heavenly Father, thank you for providing all that I need for life and godliness. I admit that (include anything that might interfere with your relationship with God) sometimes gets in the way of my growing in you. I give that to you and ask that you would guide me and help me to be diligent and seek a closer more knowledgeable relationship with you. Give me all that I need to be a beacon to others as I move through the harshness of life. In Jesus' name I pray, Amen."

2 Corinthians 9:8
New International Version 1984 (NIV1984)

8 And God is able to make all grace abound to you, so that in all things at all times, having all that you need, you will abound in every good work.

Paraphrase this scripture (put it into your own words and try to include your name as if God were speaking directly to you):

God can do so much through His work of grace within us. His grace is everywhere in our lives. As believers, we have access to God's grace for all of our needs. God, however, also supplies us with grace that He intends for us to pass on to others.

God gives us abounding grace so that we will have all we need in order to abound in good works. Now, be careful with how you define "all that you need". God knows exactly what you "need", and that may differ from what you "want". It is not sinful to want things in life. It is sinful when those desires get in the way of your relationship with your Savior. Know this, God is always providing all that you need, in order to give others what He knows they lack. Plus, God grows us through giving just as much as He grows others through receiving.

What is God, in His boundless grace, giving you that He wants you to then give to others? Has He given you money, time, wisdom, love, compassion, a shoulder to cry on, a book to write, a study to lead, a job to do, friendship, trust through hard times, joy, and on and on. The list is endless.

If you are faithful to do this, God will cause you to abound in every good work. You will find that the more you give the more you have to give. Doing this will not necessarily give you what you want, but God will always provide what He knows you need. You will also find that your giving to others will do more for your own walk with Christ than you ever dreamed.

Personal Touch:

What is God gracing you with that you could turn and give to others?

What have you been thinking of doing for the Lord but have been afraid to attempt?

Who can you grace today with the abundance you have been given?

Prayer:

"Dear Heavenly Father, thank you for providing for all of my needs through your abundant grace. I know that fear of (include whatever keeps you from stepping out of your comfort zone) keeps me from doing all that you desire me to do. I give you that fear, and I pray that you would fill me with your grace to do all that you place before me today. Make me sensitive to each situation and tender my heart to the needs of others. I thank you for the privilege of serving others in your name. In Jesus' name I pray, Amen."

1 Peter 5:10
New International Version 1984 (NIV1984)

10 And the God of all grace, who called you to his eternal glory in Christ, after you have suffered a little while, will himself restore you and make you strong, firm and steadfast.

Paraphrase this scripture (put it into your own words and try to include your name as if God were speaking directly to you):

The God of all grace has called you into eternal glory with Christ. Pause for a second and read that again. All grace is from God, and through it He has saved you. As a believer you are an heir to eternity in heaven. This is wonderful, and changes how we view life, but we have not entered heaven just yet.

Even though we are called to this ultimate eternity, God does not mislead us. He is clear that while we are here on earth, we will suffer. But this God of all grace provides for that as well. He has determined that our suffering here will be for just a little while. It may seem like an eternity of tribulation, but God has His hand on what He allows into your life. It will be just as much as is needed for His purposes in your life and in the lives of those around you. He is in control and what you are going through will never gain the upper hand

This God of all grace will also restore you. The God of the Universe is concerned and cares about you so much that He Himself will provide this for you. Now, you will not be restored to the same person you were before your time of suffering began. You may be different physically and/or life may be very different than it was before. But God will grow you and make you strong, firm and steadfast. Each trial is an opportunity to come out on the other side with the deep imprint of God all over you.

This is a promise from God. We know that we will suffer, but He promises that He will restore us and make us stronger for Him. Depend on Him. Seek Him and know that you will find the grace that He is promising.

Personal Touch:

Has God ever provided restoration for you? What did it look like?

How can you face trials so that you are left with the imprint of God?

Do you need restoration today? How can you use this verse to guide you through?

Prayer:

"Dear Heavenly Father, thank you for being the God of all grace and providing all that I need as I suffer through this life here on earth. Help me to be eternally minded, and help me to be a willing vessel for your glory. Restore me and make me all that you desire me to be, even if that is different from what I am now. I take comfort in this promise and praise you for the restoration that is yet to come. In Jesus' name I pray, Amen."

Acts 4:33
New International Version 1984 (NIV1984)

33 With great power the apostles continued to testify to the resurrection of the Lord Jesus, and much grace was upon them all.

Paraphrase this scripture (put it into your own words and try to include your name as if God were speaking directly to you):

As Christians, our main purpose for being here on Earth is to share the gospel. This happens in a number of ways. It can be through direct verbal instruction but more often we show Christ to others through how we live our lives. We are also given spiritual gifts to use in our daily walk. How we share the gospel can vary. What should not be in question is our ability to accomplish what God has asked of us. God never asks us to do something without equipping us for the job.

This passage tells us that the apostles continued to speak about the resurrection of Jesus. They spoke with great power, conviction, resolution, and courage. They were empowered to do what God called them to do through His grace. How much grace? Much grace was given. They were prepared for their calling through the grace of God.

What is your calling? Maybe you know exactly what you are supposed to be doing right now, and maybe you are not quite sure. One thing we do know is that our words and our life should be pictures of Christ for others to hear and see. Whatever you do, do it with eternity in mind. Tap into the power that God wants to provide for you through His grace. Stay in His word and on your knees in prayer.

God wants you to find His will for your life. He is not keeping it a secret. It might not look like you think it should (for example, waiting is often His will but rarely something we envision as useful). Sometimes God even uses our "failures" for His will because they fit within the larger picture. Submit and obey and you will find much grace upon you to accomplish all that He sets before you.

Personal Touch:

List one thing that you know is God's will for you today.

What might impede your ability to carry out God's will?

What can you do to ensure that today is filled with much grace?

Prayer:

"Dear Heavenly Father, thank you for never asking me to do something that you don't also provide the means to accomplish. Lord, I confess that (include something that has been getting in the way of your relationship with God) has been getting in the way of our closeness. Help me to get back in tune with you and fill me with much grace to do what you have placed before me today. May I be of use to you! In Jesus name I pray, Amen."

2 Thessalonians 2:15-17
New International Version 1984 (NIV1984)

15 So then, brothers, stand firm and hold to the teachings we passed on to you, whether by word of mouth or by letter.
16 May our Lord Jesus Christ himself and God our Father, who loved us and by his grace gave us eternal encouragement and good hope, 17 encourage your hearts and strengthen you in every good deed and word.

Paraphrase this scripture (put it into your own words and try to include your name as if God were speaking directly to you):

Stand firm. When your life is sunny, stand firm. When your life is threatened by a storm, stand firm. In either situation, it can be more difficult than it might look to stand firm in Christ. When life is plugging along and all is good, it is easy to forget your need for God. During the hard times it is easy to become angry with God or simply rely on self in an attempt to gain a semblance of control.

God, in His great love for us, does not leave us without what we need to stand firm in Him. He never asks us to do something without providing the means to accomplish it. Because of His love, and through His grace, He has given us eternal encouragement and good hope. This is a rock on which to build your life so that you will stand firm. You are loved, chosen, saved, set apart and will spend eternity with Christ. This is the certainty upon which to stand firm no matter what the weather of your current existence.

God will encourage your hearts and strengthen you for every good deed and word. This prayer does not ask, or say, that God will change the circumstances of your life. It says that His love and grace will change the circumstances of your heart. He will strengthen and encourage you so that you can accomplish His will despite the situation. Through Him and His grace you can stand firm.

Personal Touch:

What does it look like to stand firm in Christ?

How has God encouraged and strengthened you to stand firm in the past?

What can you do today to help ensure that your foundation is firm in Christ rather than anything else?

Prayer:

"Dear Heavenly Father, thank you for providing the means to stand firm no matter what my circumstances might be. I confess that (include anything that distracts you from God) often pulls me away from my firm walk with you. Help me to stand firm in (include any struggles). Be my source of encouragement, hope, and strength. Help me to tap into this so that I will say and do all that you desire of me today. In Jesus' name I pray, Amen."

* 9 7 8 0 6 1 5 9 4 3 6 6 4 *